Antoine Augustin Parmentier

Observations on such nutritive vegetables

As may be substituted in the place of ordinary food in times of scarcity

Antoine Augustin Parmentier

Observations on such nutritive vegetables
As may be substituted in the place of ordinary food in times of scarcity

ISBN/EAN: 9783742811783

Manufactured in Europe, USA, Canada, Australia, Japa

Cover: Foto ©Gila Hanssen / pixelio.de

Manufactured and distributed by brebook publishing software (www.brebook.com)

Antoine Augustin Parmentier

Observations on such nutritive vegetables

OBSERVATIONS

ON SUCH

NUTRITIVE VEGETABLES

AS MAY BE SUBSTITUTED IN THE
PLACE OF

ORDINARY FOOD.

[Price 1*s.* 6*d.*]

NUTRITIVE VEGETABLES

AS MAY BE SUBSTITUTED IN THE PLACE OF

ORDINARY FOOD,

IN TIMES OF SCARCITY.

EXTRACTED FROM THE FRENCH OF
M. PARMENTIER.

Fas est vel ab hoste doceri.

LONDON:
PRINTED FOR J. MURRAY, FLEET-STREET.

MDCCLXXXIII.

PREFACE,

BY THE TRANSLATOR.

AT the present period of scarcity and dearness of provisions, when the common people have been already excited to discontent and tumult, by the distress that has so soon begun to press upon them, and by the prospect of the still deeper distress in which they will probably be involved before another harvest; and when, besides a great army and fleet, distant islands are to be maintained out of stores, perhaps little more than sufficient for home-consumption; it is incumbent upon every man to propose publicly whatever means he may suppose likely to avert or alleviate the impending calamities.

There are perhaps few publications better calculated to promote so desirable an end than the

the Essay of M. PARMENTIER, *which gained the prize proposed by the Academy of Besançon, in* 1777; *and appeared in* 1780, *considerably enlarged and improved, under the title of* "Recherches sur les vegetaux nourrissans qui dans le temps de disette, &c."

The author is advantageously known by several works, in which the skill of the Philosopher is united with the benevolence of the Citizen of the World: his Treatise on the Chesnut, his Perfect Baker, his Oeconomical Essay on Potatoes, and the book above-mentioned, are so many instances of the ardour and success with which he has laboured in the service of the most numerous, and therefore the most valuable class of society.

The frequent and severe attacks of scarcity, and even of famine, felt in France, render researches like M. PARMENTIER's an object of the highest national importance; and, unhappily, the present year has afforded ample proof, that no fertility of soil, or skill in husbandry, can absolutely secure any nation against such disasters.

As the Work from which the following observations are extracted, has been well received by the judicious and humane in every part of Europe, it will probably be asked why it was not published entire, rather than in its present mutilated form? The answer is not difficult, and it is hoped will be satisfactory. The author has entered into so many minute investigations, both chemical and physiological, as to render his Work not only too bulky for those for whose benefit the present publication is designed, but above their comprehension: such details can be interesting to the physician and philosopher only; whereas general utility is the object of the following pages: in this view, the articles relating to the matter of nutriment—to the constituent parts of corn—the numerous objections to Potatoes, and bread of Potatoes, with the answers—besides many others, have been omitted: and with the part that has been retained, considerable liberties have been taken;

for

for every paragraph and sentence, which did not convey some useful information, has been suppressed.

Whether any of the preparations pointed out by M. PARMENTIER may be useful to the navy; or whether they deserve to be enumerated among those visionary projects, which every day obtrude upon the attention of those who fill high and important offices in the state, let the ministers of the marine determine. Should Potatoes be found, on further trial, to possess the antiscorbutic virtues of late attributed to them, they will become an object hardly less interesting in times of the greatest plenty than in those of scarcity, especially since a mode of preserving them to any length of time has been discovered. The cultivation of them, already carried to a great height, cannot be too much encouraged; for, as M. PARMENTIER observes, (and the present season furnishes a remarkable instance of the truth of his observation) the years most unfavourable to grain yield the most abundant crops of this valuable root.

Dec. 1782.

OBSERVATIONS, &c.

CHAPTER I.

OF THE USE OF POTATOES IN SUBSTANCE.

AMONG Potatoes there are infinite varieties of colour, bulk, shape, consistence, and taste: but these varieties are not always, as it hath been pretended, the effect of soil, season, and care bestowed in cultivation; they arise from a real difference of species; for there are corresponding differences in the parts of fructification; the flowers being sometimes of a cineritious grey and dirty white, and sometimes of a pale red or fine blue; the verdure of the leaves, the stalk and fruit, are also subject to varieties; there are both early and late Potatoes: it neverthelefs appears that the conftituent parts of the roots are always of the fame nature, differing only in proportion.

ALTHOUGH the good effects of Potatoes in fubftance are fully proved by the daily ufe which whole nations and feveral of our own provinces make of them, yet they have not efcaped the fhafts of calumny. How many imaginary evils have been imputed to them! How many forged tales would have been circulated againft them, if a multitude of writers, well qualified to decide concerning the effects produced by food in the animal œconomy, had not defended and juftified that which is afforded by thefe roots! It was on fuch an occafion that the Faculty of Medicine at Paris being confulted by the Comptroller-general on the wholefomenefs of Potatoes, charged with caufing difeafes in fome of our provinces, made a report highly favourable to them, and well calculated to diffipate all apprehenfions.

BUT

But as it would be infufficient to remind prejudiced perfons, that in the moft populous provinces of Germany many millions of men fubfift almoft entirely on this food; or to quote the remark of an excellent obferver concerning the Irifh, whofe chief nourifhment confifts of Potatoes:— (The Irifh, fays he, are robuft: they are ftrangers to many difeafes by which other nations are afflicted; nothing is more common than to meet with perfons advanced in years, and to fee twins playing about the hut of the peafant.)—I conceived, that in order to quiet all alarms, and to remove every fubterfuge of prejudice, it would be neceffary to enter upon fome chemical difcuffions and enquiries.

I therefore proved, by a long train of experiments, that Potatoes in their natural ftate contained three diftinct and effential principles, when each was examined by itfelf; *viz.* 1. a dry powder, refembling the ftarch contained in grain; 2. a light fibrous matter, of a grey colour, and of the fame same nature as that contained in the roots of pot-herbs; 3. lastly, a mucilaginous juice, which has no peculiar properties, but may be compared to the juice of succulent plants, such as borage and buglofs.

I NEXT distilled Potatoes in a retort; they gave out an immense quantity of water, which towards the end of the operation became more and more acid; next there passed a light and an heavy oil, resembling that generally obtained from the parts of plants containing flour. A pound of these roots leaves scarce 36 grains of earthy residuum which has all the characters of vegetable earth.

WHAT effects then are produced by the boiling which these roots are made to undergo before they are eaten? It tends to combine these different principles more intimately, and to form a whole more soluble and of easier digestion. To divide the Potatoes afterwards by means of a grater, and to set them under the prefs, would

would be to little purpose: it would be impossible to express a single drop of water, or to precipitate a particle of starch.

It is well known that the vessel in which Potatoes have been boiled is by that operation coloured green, and they sometimes leave behind them a slight acrimony sufficiently sensible to the throat: now these circumstances afforded sufficient scope to the vilifiers of this valuable plant, to impute several diseases to it: but I further proved that these two properties do not belong to the whole of the root, but only to the red skin by which it is covered externally, and that several other roots present the same phænomena, such as radishes, which lose their colour as fast as they come in contact with boiling water, tinging it with a green hue, and at the same time parting with their well-known pungency; and lastly, that this colouring matter with which the skin of the Potatoe furnishes water, is simply extractive, and contains nothing virulent or saline.

Besides,

Besides, how can this green colour be noxious, when roasted Potatoes, which retain it, are as wholesome as boiled? nay, they are more savoury and delicate; an advantage arising from the dissipation of the aqueous fluid, and perhaps from the same extractive matter which communicates the green colour to water.

Some of the advocates for Potatoes, alarmed by this green colour, and persuaded that it exists in their juice, have proposed to extract it, and substitute water in its stead; but there cannot perhaps be a more absurd proposal. In our islands the juice of the mangoe is separated because it is really poisonous; I have also imitated the process of the Americans in several indigenous, farinaceous roots, which without this previous extraction would be very dangerous: but the juice of the Potatoe is far from containing any thing similar; like all the other principles, it is essential to it when we would eat it in substance. In order to separate it, the aggregation must

must be broken, the fibrous nets must be torn in pieces, and the expressed residuum be employed only in the form of pap; which, instead of adding to the wholesomeness of Potatoes, would make an insipid, heavy, and indigestible food.

THE vegetable kingdom affords no food more wholesome, more easily procured, or less expensive, than the Potatoe. It is well known with what resources it furnished the Irish in 1740; many families would have been swept away without this supply: the eagerness with which children devour it, the preference which they give it to the chesnut, would seem to shew that it is well adapted to the constitution of man: persons of all ages and temperaments feed upon it without experiencing the slightest inconvenience. In the last German war these roots were the resource of many soldiers, who happening to be separated from the main body of the army, would have fallen sacrifices to fatigue and hunger, if they had not met with Potatoes, which they eat in exceffive quantities after fimple boiling, and with no other feafoning than a good appetite: gratitude induced feveral of them to import the plant into their own country, where it was unknown: they cultivated it with fkill, and fet an example which was foon imitated. At prefent there is fcarce an elegant repaft where Potatoes are not introduced with emulation in various difguifes; and the great confumption in the Capital, proves that they are no longer defpifed there.

The exceffive price to which grain has been advanced of late years, forms a remarkable æra at which the beneficial qualities of Potatoes have been begun to be tried in many places. An officer of diftinction, while he was improving one of his eftates, grew a great quantity of Potatoes, but being well acquainted with the ftubbornnefs of ruftic prejudices, he was aware that the eloquence of example would be infinitely more perfuafive than whatever he could fay: he had five dogs, a yard well
ftocked

stocked with poultry of every sort, twenty cows, and two pigs, to feed daily: he explained to his servants his intention of nourishing all the animals with Potatoes alone; by which means the grain which they would have consumed might be employed for the service of men. His orders were punctually obeyed, because the punishment of disobedience was the dismission of the first who was guilty of it. Pretending afterwards that the Potatoe was difficult of digestion, he forbade his servants to eat them. These contrivances produced the expected effect, and thus he made this plant an object of attention in his neighbourhood.

If we consider all the properties of Potatoes, we shall be forced to acknowledge, that if there really exists a medicinal food, it is to be found in these roots. All the English authors who have spoken of Potatoes, regard them as light and very nutritious. Ellis, who paid great attention to the culture of them, bestows the most pompous

pompous epithets upon them, and announces them as the food of all others moſt ſuitable to his countrymen, on account of their general practice of eating great quantities of fleſh. Lemery in his Treatiſe on Food, and Tiſſot in his Eſſay on the Diſeaſes of People of Faſhion, agree in recommending ſtrongly the uſe of Potatoes: But I will ſelect a few obſervations from the great number of which I can anſwer for the truth, by way of reply to the objections that have been brought againſt Potatoes.

M. Engel in his Inſtructions how to cultivate the Potatoe, informs us, that ſeveral of his friends who had lived three years almoſt on Potatoes alone, experienced no inconvenience, and were far from being ſatiated: among others he mentions a maiden lady 33 years of age, who was in ſo bad a ſtate of health, that her appetite was quite gone and her ſtomach incapable of digeſting any thing, when ſhe happened to take a fancy to live on Potatoes; ſhe experienced ſuch happy effects from this diet,

diet, as to recover her gaiety, plumpnefs, and appetite in a fhort time.

A merchant of a very ftrong conftitution was fo reduced by an illnefs of nine months continuance, that he voided his food juft as he took it; one day he thought of eating Potatoes, by which he was fo much benefited, that he declared to me that the good ftate of health which he now enjoyed was owing to them alone.

I had a relation of a keen appetite, and in the habit of ufing conftant exercife: he could not eat the feeds of any leguminous plant without being afterwards tormented by the heart-burn, but found that Potatoes never produced any fuch effect. I know fome perfons who live on milk and Potatoes alone, not being able to digeft any other food: I am acquainted with others who have been cured of a fcorbutic taint by the moderate ufe of Potatoes; their ftomach, fo far from being weakened, acquired greater ftrength and vigour.

These

These observations, which might easily be multiplied, and which are confirmed by my analysis of Potatoes, prove how far these roots ought to be exempted from all suspicion of lying heavy on the stomach of those who use them for food, since every pound contains 11½ ounces of water, and the 4½ ounces of solid parts remaining, afford scarce a drachm of earth.

Another objection still subsisting in force against the wholesomeness of Potatoes is, that as they belong to the family of Solanum, they must needs possess narcotic properties; but experience has long since shewn how little such botanical analogies are to be depended on. Is it not well known that the family of convolvulus, which is in general acrimonious, pungent, and caustic, and supplies medicine with its most drastic purgatives, affords in the Batatta a mild saccharine aliment, which, to be used for food, needs only to be boiled? It is indeed true that some observations with which I have been favoured, seem to shew

shew a soporific virtue in the Potatoe; and, as I have no interest in concealing any thing, I will set them down here.

A domestic of the Baron de St. Hilaire, after a malignant fever could not recover his sleep: his master ordered him to sup on Potatoes; and that very night he slept six hours without intermission: the continuance of the same practice produced the same effect, without causing any change in his constitution.

Mr. M. of a meagre habit, but of an uninterrupted good state of health, during two years made constant use of roasted Potatoes, seasoned with a little butter and salt; having been always before accustomed to eat very sparingly at his evening meal, he acquired from relish the habit of eating six or seven of the largest Potatoes for supper: it is proper to remark, that he ate bread in proportion: he never experienced any inconvenience from this practice; but what induced him to abandon it was, that

being

being obliged to rife early, he suppofed that his sleep was more profound, and that he awaked with greater difficulty; he however thinks that thefe effects arofe from the excefs, and that he fhould have experienced the fame thing from any other fupper, exceeding the bounds of moderation. When he eats Potatoes he is not fenfible of any change in his ftate of body.

I ADDUCE this laft obfervation with the greater pleafure, becaufe, the philofopher who is the fubject of it, may be quoted as an authority in medicine. If excefs in this food induces fleepinefs, what other excefs would not be attended with more pernicious confequences? if we even fuppofe this foporific virtue to be inherent in the Potatoe, continual ufe will make it quite ineffectual, as it happens to all kinds of aliment, which have been fuppofed, on no better grounds to poffefs particular properties. The quantity of water contained in Potatoes, may moderate the effervefcence of the blood,

blood, by giving it a greater degree of consistence, but without rendering it at the same time more viscid.

The property which of all others renders the Potatoe so valuable in the country, is, according to the testimony of the faculty of medicine at Paris, its improving the quality and encreasing the quantity of the milk of animals: it produced this effect on the nurses of the poor infants of the parish of St. Roch: at least the physicians of this parish, in their printed certificate, attest that this food is not only more wholesome than any other procurable by the poor, but likewise that it prevents many diseases to which children are subject, and by which great numbers are cut off, such as ulcers, diseases of the eyes, atrophy, &c.

CHAPTER

CHAPTER II.

OF THE USE OF POTATOES, IN BREAD.

WHILST Potatoes were considered in France only as an additional article to the luxury of our tables, their usefulness as a food was little attended to; they did not become a serious object till the possibility of converting them into bread, that is to say, of increasing the quantity of that prepared from the flour of different grains, was perceived. I must own, that in 1771, when I was analysing these roots, I had this object in view; persuaded that in the form of bread they would be an useful supplement in times of scarcity of grain, and that at all times it would be a sure way of making it serve from one harvest to another in those districts where Potatoes are much cultivated; and by these means also they might be appropriated for food when they could no longer be eaten in substance.

It was scarce found that Potatoes mixed with common dough, are made to disappear, by means of kneading, so as to form an homogeneous and well-raised mass, when these roots were believed to be changed into real bread. Enthusiasm laid hold of men's minds; different methods were proposed, each person boasting his own: the consequence was, that many, misled by a deceitful appearance, have asserted, and even now repeat, that they have prepared, seen or eaten bread made of Potatoes; they have even gone so far as to dispute for the honour of the invention; though the Irish had recourse to this substitute almost as soon as they began to make use of Potatoes. Their attempts are preserved in several parts of the Philosophical Transactions; to which I refer those who may yet cherish the hope of advancing any claims relating to this point: I would at the same time beg them not to confound any longer, bread in which Potatoes are introduced, and that confifting of thefe roots alone and unmixed!

First attempts, however imperfect, are always received with joy, efpecially when the fubftance in queftion has any connection with the fubfiftence of the moft indigent clafs of citizens; but even with the moft upright intentions it feldom happens that the advantages that may be derived are not exaggerated. To introduce into dough compofed of flour, leaven, and water, $\frac{1}{3}$ or $\frac{1}{2}$ of a watery root, without at all prejudicing the product, was a moft agreeable profpect, when confidered in an œconomical view: that the faving was not in proportion to the quantity of the fubftitute employed, could be learned only from experience.

Another circumftance not attended to, and which neverthelefs deferved attention, was, that the pulp of Potatoes mixed with wheat dough, fo much increafes the mechanical effect of the glutinous part of that

that grain, that it swells too much during the preparation and in the oven; hence the bread is extremely light, continues but a short time in the stomach, and passes too soon into the lower intestines.

Should we admit that half the weight of this bread consists of Potatoes, it will not follow that the nourishment is increased in the same proportion; there can be at most but one part, of which the nutritious effect is equivalent to an equal quantity of flour of wheat: let me confirm this by an instance;—suppose two pastes of an equal consistence, the one consisting of 4 pounds of pulp of Potatoes, and as much flour of wheat, the other of flour of the same grain unmixed; the first will afford less bread; this bread will contain more water, and will not be so nutritive as the second mass, because the Potatoe can furnish but one-third at most of its weight in farinaceous matter, that can be compared with the flour of grains; the surplus is nothing but the water of vegetation, which keeps the principles of thefe roots at a diftance from each other, and in a ftate of great divifion.

With refpect to the difappearance of Potatoes in the above-mentioned mixture, this phænomenon ought to caufe no more furprize than others of daily occurrence; as for inftance, when pulpous fruits, fuch as the pumpion, gourd, the herbaceous ftalks of plants, the flefhy roots, are added to flour of wheat, ought it to be concluded that all fubftances which, without being farinaceous, can be fo affimilated with dough as not to be diftinguifhable except by the organ of tafte, are transformed into bread? or that when the mafs has been increafed two-fold, and even three-fold, the nutritive virtue has received an equal augmentation? Several facts prove the contrary: and the inhabitants of the Pays de Vaud, among others, who have been much accuftomed to eat this mixed bread, complain that the appetite is not eafily fatisfied with it.

It

It would undoubtedly be wrong to infer from this obfervation, that the prefence of Potatoes is capable of impairing the nutritive effects of the fubftances to which they are added, and of confequence that the practice of mixing them with the flour of different grains ought to be difcontinued; but let me repeat it once more, they can nourifh only in proportion to the quantity of fubftantial matter which they contain; and it would be ridiculous to require as much nourifhment from a watery root as from a dry feed, which in order to be ufed as a food, muft previoufly be combined with a fluid.

If there are particular circumftances in which recourfe fhould be had to the fupplement of Potatoes for the preparation of white bread, it muft be when the quantity of wheat is not in proportion to the confumption. As it is the common food of the rich and the inhabitants of cities, it is of little importance whether it is more or lefs fubftantial; in general it is only an addition to other meats: but this does not hold with refpect to the brown meal of the fame grain; it has not fo much vifcidity as the white; the mixture of Potatoes gives it more bulk, lightnefs and quality.

Next to wheat, rye is the moft valuable grain; both, mixed or feparate, afford, if well prepared, a very excellent bread, without the neceffity of any addition: but when they are fcarce, and brought from a great diftance, and very dear, the Potatoe, if there is a fufficient ftock, would make a faving of other grains, which ferve the moft indigent clafs.

If it is important to fet bounds to the practice of ufing Potatoes to enlarge the bulk of wheat and rye bread; it is proper to remark, that this practice is extremely wholefome for barley, buck-wheat, maize, oats, millet, &c, with which bread is prepared in different diftricts of the realm; for this bread, whether compofed of the meal

meal pure or mixed, is conftantly heavy, clofe, and ill-tafted. In this cafe the addition of an equal part of Potatoes would occafion very defirable changes in thefe feveral kinds, by giving tenacity and vifcidity to the dough, by promoting the fermentative motion, by weakening and even deftroying the difagreeable tafte peculiar to each of them.

In the prefent cafe, not only the quantity of bread will be increafed, but the quality will be improved; a great advantage for the poor in general, and even for whole diftricts, which confume only thefe kinds of grains. For the fake of this clafs of people, it will be proper to point out a method by which the grain may be faved and the bread improved. In this view, I will give a receipt for the compofition of this bread; it will ferve as a model for every other propofed to be made in this way with all farinaceous fubftances indifcriminately, provided they are in a proper ftate for making bread:

TAKE

Take any quantity of Potatoes, well crushed and bruised; mix them with the leaven prepared the evening before in the usual way, with the whole of the flour designed for making the dough, so that one-half may consist of pulp of Potatoes and half of flour; knead the whole with the necessary quantity of warm water; when the dough is sufficiently prepared, put it in the oven, taking care not to heat it so much as usual, not to shut it up so soon, and to leave it longer in; without this essential precaution, the crust of the bread would be hard and short, while the inside would have too much moisture and not be soaked enough.

Whenever it is proposed to mix Potatoes with the dough of different grains, either to save a part or to improve the bread, these roots should be reduced into the form of a glutinous paste, because in this state they give tenacity to the flour of small grain, which are always deficient in this respect.

The other ways of preparing Potatoes before mixing them with the flour, are not nearly so advantageous as boiling them: these ways may be reduced to two principal ones: according to the first, they are taken raw and grated; here they are employed without losing any part of their juice and skin: the second consists in cutting them in slices, then baking, and afterwards taking them to the mill: but the bread in both cases is dark-coloured, close, and ill-tasted.

Were all these methods even less defective than they are in reality, they do not obtain the end proposed; *viz.* saving the expence of boiling, and the other operations; for it will cost at least as much to grate or dry the Potatoes: it is not only necessary to boil, but also to crush and manage them so as to give them the consistence and form of a tenacious and viscid paste, in order that they may produce the effects above described.

LET me recapitulate. It cannot be doubted, that if wheat and rye were very fcarce, and their high price obliged men to feek a fupplement in other grains, it would be better to have recourfe to a mixture of Potatoes: they may befides ferve to give other grains a fuperior degree of goodnefs. It is well known, that in times of dearth, neceffity, incapable of making any enquiries when exceffive, always guides the hand to objects ill calculated to fulfil our intentions, and productive of effects the moft oppofite to our wifhes.

BUT, in circumftances affording no other means of fubfiftence but Potatoes in plenty, the converfion of them into bread would be advantageous, becaufe there are multitudes fo habituated to live upon bread, that they would not believe that their appetite was fatisfied, if food was offered them in any other form.

I COME now to defcribe the preparation,

tion, which is to serve as a basis for all the farinaceous plants, afterwards to be pointed out as proper to supply the place of our common aliments when they fail.

CHAPTER III.

OF THE WAY TO MAKE BREAD OF POTATOES, WITHOUT MIXTURE.

PREVIOUS to any attempts to convert the farinaceous parts of plants into bread, it is necessary to prepare them by certain preliminary operations: the intention of these operations is to dispose their constituent parts to unite with water, and thus to give them a degree of softness and flexibility, favourable to the fermentative motion which is to take place among them. Such is the chief end of the process which I am now to describe; it naturally precedes the task of the baker, in the fabrication of any bread whatever.

Of the Starch of Potatoes.

AFTER having repeatedly wafhed the Potatoes, in order to feparate the dirt and fand, divide them by a grater of tin fet in a wooden frame and refting on a fearce; empty it when full into a larger veffel: the grated Potatoe affords a liquid pafte, which grows darker coloured on being expofed to the air; pour fome water on this pafte, and ftir it about with a ftick or your hands, and pour the whole into a fearce placed over another veffel; the turbid water which paffes through, carries the ftarch along with it, and depofits it at the bottom of the veffel: the reddifh water is to be thrown away, and frefh quantities are to be added till it is no longer tinged.

AFTER this firft operation, the procefs of the Starch-maker fhould be exactly imitated; the precipitate, when well wafhed, is to be taken out, divided into parcels, and

and set upon searces or boards exposed to the sun in order to dissipate the excess of moisture; as it dries, the dirty grey colour changes to a shining white: this substance is real starch, and by being sifted through close searces, acquires a tenuity equal to that of the finest starch of wheat.

What remains on the searce, although deprived both of starch and extractive matter, may serve, like bran, for feeding cattle: it may also be reduced to powder, for a purpose which I shall have occasion to mention in speaking of the brown bread of Potatoes. There are situations where nothing should be lost, especially of the objects of immediate necessity.

Remarks.

The most important observation that occurs here, is, that Potatoes, to whatever variety they may belong, and in whatever condition they may happen to be when they are used, provided they are raw, constantly ftantly afford ftarch, differing only in quantity; hence Potatoes fpoiled by froft, germination, or too ripe, may be ufed for this purpofe.

If it fhould be requifite to employ the ftarch immediately, and circumftances not allowing time to provide a ftock, or to wait till it can be dried and paffed through the fearce, it may be ufed as foon as it is feparated; but the water, which conftitutes about one-half of its weight, fhould be deducted. I even think that I have obferved, that in its wet ftate it renders the dough a little more tenacious, and the bread whiter.

It is neceffary to break the aggregation of the integrant parts, to tear in pieces the fibrous nets, and to force the ftarch contained in them to quit its place of refidence: wherefore an inftrument calculated only to flice or bruife thefe roots, would be quite ufelefs in the prefent cafe.

To

To thefe obfervations let me add, that though all forts of Potatoes are capable of being changed into bread, the round, grey ones afford moft ftarch; every pound produces nearly from two to three ounces: but as I have already remarked, the feafon, foil, and cultivation, have great influence in this refpect.

Of the Pulp of Potatoes.

As foon as the Potatoes are well baked or boiled, they fhould be peeled, and then crufhed with a rolling-pin or the hand upon a table. Scarce have they loft their form, when they begin to ftick together and to form a pafte, which grows more and more elaftic and fpungy, without the neceffity of adding any fluid: this procefs is to be continued till every lump is broken; then it is to be fet afide: and the whole fhould be thus reduced.

As Potatoes do not acquire the tenacity of a pulp but whilft they are yet warm, and

and as by a neceſſary conſequence the pulp itſelf loſes its viſcidity as it grows cold, the trouble of boiling theſe roots ſeveral times a day may be avoided, by putting them, boiled and peeled, to ſoak a ſhort time in the hot water deſigned for kneading: by theſe means they are made to regain under the rolling-pin their viſcidity; a quality eſſential and indiſpenſable in the fabrication of bread.

The pulp of Potatoes may be kept two days and longer, according to the ſeaſon, without danger of ſpoiling. It then indeed is not ſo tenacious, and does not ſo nearly reſemble the glutinous matter of wheat; and it is of the greateſt importance that it ſhould bear the ſtrongeſt reſemblance to this matter, both in tenacity and elaſticity, the other chemical properties in which theſe two ſubſtances differ from each other, being totally inſignificant in the making of bread.

Remarks.

Remarks.

It is with Potatoes as with the roots of pot-herbs and leguminous feeds: the nature of the water has a fingular influence on the fuccefs and quicknefs of the boiling. The hardnefs of the water may be diminifhed by boiling. But Potatoes fhould never be drowned, nor fhould the veffel which contains them be ever uncovered, becaufe the water, after it has been reduced into vapour, fhould be driven back, in order the better to infinuate itfelf into the texture of each tubercle, to penetrate and combine more perfectly its conftituent parts; in confequence of which they are fooner boiled and more favoury. This obfervation holds with refpect to all vegetable, flefhy, and aqueous fubftances, which ought not when they are boiled to be drowned with water, unlefs they contain a matter neceffary to be extracted, and in that cafe too much water cannot be employed.

I HAVE obferved, that the preparation of ftarch admitted indifferently every fort of Potatoes in every poffible ftate; but we cannot hope for the fame advantages in obtaining the pulp; this preparation requires choice; the red fort feems to afford the moft tenacious and elaftic pafte, and confequently merits preference: it is of great importance that they fhould be found and free from defects.

IT would be impoffible to make bread of Potatoes without the aid of the pulp, fince it is that alone which gives tenacity and vifcidity to the ftarch, which is quite deftitute of thefe qualities.

Of the Leaven of Potatoes.

MIX half a pound of pulp of Potatoes with an equal quantity of the ftarch, and four ounces of boiling water; fet the mixture in a warm place: in forty-eight hours a flight vinous fmell fhould be exhaled from it; and now a frefh portion of ftarch, starch, pulp, and water, should be added, and the mass again exposed to the same temperature for the same space of time: this operation should yet be repeated a third time. The paste thus gradually turned sour may be considered as a first leaven.

In the evening dilute this first leaven with warm water, mix equal parts of starch and pulp in the proportion of one half of the dough, so that for every twenty pounds of dough ten of leaven must be prepared; when the mixture is exactly made, put it in a basket, or leave it in the kneading tub all night, taking care to cover it well, and to keep it warm till morning.

Remarks.

The tedious and troublesome preparation of the first leaven will be avoided after the first baking, because a piece of the dough may be set aside and kept.

The trouble attending the preparation of this firſt leaven, may be avoided by introducing at the firſt baking ſome leaven of dough or yeaſt, without the neceſſity of mixing the ſtarch and pulp; I will even obſerve, that it does not gain the character of good leaven, till ſome time after its formation: this law is common to every leaven prepared in the ſame manner, even to that of wheat, for the bread is always ſtiff and heavy when ſuch a leaven is firſt uſed. My motive for pointing out ſo long a proceſs was, to prove that the Potatoe was capable of ſerving for the elements of leaven, and that, like grain, it might be made to undergo the bread fermentation, without the aid of any foreign agent.

Of the dough of Potatoes.

In order to prepare the dough, the leaven ſhould be ſet in the middle of the ſtarch, ſurrounded by the pulp, divided into pieces; it ſhould be diluted with ſome warm water, to which half a drachm of salt for every pound of the mixture should be added; and when the whole is confounded by kneading, it should be subjected to the different operations proper to increase its viscidity and tenacity; that is to say, it should be lifted up, gathered and beaten; but the fifts should not be thrust into it, which is a very general but very bad practice in the making of bread of all forts.

As soon as the paste is kneaded it should be divided and formed into loaves of a proper size, which should be set in tin moulds, sprinkled over with bran or starch, to prevent the adhesion of the dough, which generally takes place without this precaution: the moulds should be covered with a wet cloth, and left in a warm place for two or three hours, according to the season.

REMARKS.

As it is easy to obtain bread of different degrees of consistence, by only varying the quantity

quantity of water ufed for kneading, it follows that it may alfo be obtained lighter or heavier from Potatoes, by varying the procefs in the fame manner.

THE quantity of falt may alfo be varied: the water ought always to be near the boiling point; and we need not fear left it fhould deftroy, as when wheat flour is ufed, the tenacity of the dough, on the contrary, at this temperature, it contributes to increafe it; thus the fame end is often attained by different and even oppofite means.

THE time required by the dough to attain the proper degree of fermentation cannot be exactly afcertained, becaufe it is regulated by the feafon: this muft be learned from experience: I will only remark, that it is always rather longer than that required by wheaten dough.

Of the Baking.

WHEN the leaven has been prepared the evening before, the kneading properly executed, the dough turned immediately afterwards, and diftributed in moulds, the operator fhould yet wait two or three hours before he heats his oven, and this procefs requires two hours; then the dough may be put in, after the furface has been moiftened again: it fhould be kept in the oven an hour, or two hours at moft.

REMARKS.

THE bread in queftion requires a long continued fermentation, and an oven very gently heated.

IN order to induce perfons to ufe all the precautions I lay down, it is neceffary fometimes to explain their effects: Now I recommend turning the dough as foon as it is kneaded, left while it continues in the lump its vifcidity fhould be fo far impaired as to prevent its being handled and fhaped: the furface fhould be kept moift left it fhould be fuddenly feized by the heat, and becoming hard and thick hinder the baking of the center, and the exfuding of the moifture from the foft part.

CHAPTER IV.

OF THE BREAD OF POTATOES.

BY this method I will venture to affert, from various and repeated trials, that the Potatoe, which hitherto hath not been converted into a well-raifed bread, without the mixture of at leaft an equal quantity of fome flour, may be made to affume that form without any foreign affiftance: the whole artifice confifts in fubjecting thefe roots to two previous operations

tions before the application of the ufual procefs of the baker.

BREAD of Potatoes is then compofed half of ftarch and half of pulp, with half a drachm of falt to every pound of the mixture. The water, which conftitutes about $\frac{1}{5}$ of the whole mafs, is totally diffipated during the baking; hence, in order to obtain a pound of this bread, three pounds and an half of Potatoes, *i. e.* nine ounces of ftarch, and as much pulp, are requifite. But it is of confequence to remark, that in this diminution our roots lofe only their exceffive moifture. The nutritive matter which they contain, fo far from being impaired in its effects, muft neceffarily have gained by the bread fermentation, a procefs that is well known to improve all farinaceous fubftances indifcriminately, by increafing their bulk and folubility.

IT is poffible to obtain from Potatoes a brown bread yet more œconomical. In order

order to effect this, these roots and the fibrous matter remaining on the searce after the extraction of the starch, should be dried, and then reduced to powder, with which an equal quantity of boiled Potatoes, reduced to a pulp in the manner described above, should be mixed: in this case peeling them may be dispensed with, since the kneading performed by robust arms will completely divide the skin; but this brown bread, whatever care is taken in preparing it, is always close, heavy, and ill-tasted.

Yeast diluted with water, is the proper ferment to be employed, wherever brewing is practised.

I would propose to add one-twelfth of meal in the preparation of this bread; by this means fifty pounds of grain, scarce enough for a month's sustenance, would furnish bread for the whole year.

CHAPTER

CHAPTER V.

OF THE BISCUIT OF POTATOES.

In order to prepare biscuit of Potatoes, mix a little yeast or leaven diluted with hot water, with one pound of pulp of Potatoes, and as much starch; of the whole form dough, and knead it long; after which, separate pieces of about three quarters each, and flatten them so as to leave them about twenty-four inches in circumference, and fifteen or sixteen lines in diameter.

When the dough has been thus divided and shaped, set it upon plates, and in about an hour afterwards put it in the oven, first pricking it with an iron instrument, provided with several teeth, in order to prevent it from swelling, by promoting the evaporation from every point.

As this dough contains but little water, it is more difficult to be baked; hence it muſt be left in the oven longer than the bread, for two hours at leaſt, and the rather as it ought to be baked more.

The biſcuit at its being taken out of the oven ſhould be ſet in a warm place, that it might cool gradually and be deprived of its moiſture, which is continually exhaled as long as the heat ſubſiſts. It is of great conſeqence not to pack it up under five or ſix days after it has been made, and to keep it in as dry a place as poſſible.

Biscuit of wheat in general loſes ⅓ of its weight in the oven; hence in order to obtain half a pound, ¾ of the firmeſt dough muſt be uſed. Our biſcuit undergoes a nearly equal loſs; the water employed for diluting the leaven, and which is ſufficient for kneading, is diſſipated entirely, together with a portion of that which forms a conſtituent part of the pulp.

Dif-

Different kinds of biscuit, according to the length of the voyage and the latitudes to be traversed, are prepared from wheat. In cold and dry climates biscuit is less liable to spoil; its first alteration proceeds from its attracting the moisture of the air, becoming internally mouldy, and contracting a bad smell, whence it soon becomes food for worms. This inconvenience may be always prevented, by drying the wheat perfectly, grinding it well, and not separating, as it is the practice of some places, the flour from the coarser part, *(le gruau)* which is the driest, most savoury, and most nutritious part of the grain.

The quality of biscuit does not always correspond to that of the grain of which it is made; it often depends on the process: every nation seems to have adopted one peculiar to itself; this uses a great quantity of leaven, that very little, a third none at all; and yet the taste of the biscuit depends on the quantity of leaven. As that made of Potatoes is naturally insipid,

sipid, a drachm of salt might be added to every pound, without disposing it to spoil.

The biscuit in question, when well prepared, has all the properties of common biscuit; it breaks short, is sonorous, and does not crumble on being steeped in water. The opinion of several competent judges, to whose examination it was submitted, was extremely favourable to it. The minister of the marine accepted and patronized it, observing, that the only way of learning whether it would keep as long as wheaten biscuit, was to put it on board some vessels. This direction was carefully executed; but there is every reason to apprehend that it has fallen a prey to some of the enemy's privateers.

But if I may be allowed to form a few conjectures from its appearance, and the nature of the farinaceous substance of which it consists, I think it may reasonably be presumed that it will stand long voyages;

ages; and, without defiring to fet it in compretion with common bifcuit, it feems to have one advantage over the latter, fince the Potatoe containing no faccharine or glutinous fubftance, the bifcuit made of it muft be lefs liable to attract the moifture, and confequently to fpoil.

The Potatoe grows plentifully every where, and efpecially in our iflands, of which it is a native; fo that the ineftimable advantage of victualling fhips there may be obtained, efpecially at a time of dearnefs of corn, and in circumftances when dangers at fea render communication difficult and hazardous.

I have already mentioned the antifcorbutic quality attributed by fome authors to Potatoes: Mr. MAGELLAN has lately communicated fome obfervations to the Academy of Sciences, which prove that thefe roots are really capable of curing the fcurvy: how much more probable is it then that it will prevent this difeafe, fo formidable

formidable to sailors? Thus this useful class of men would find a preservative in their daily food: it would even be desirable to put on board a certain quantity of this biscuit at all times; it would become the regimen of those whose blood shewed a tendency to scurvy.

Why should not the different kinds of Potatoe bread which I have described, and which keep sweet for a long time, be embarked on board our vessels? In order to make the experiment, two loaves newly baked, consisting of wheaten flour mixed with Potatoes, were sealed up and entrusted with a captain of a vessel ready to set sail for Spain, with an injunction to leave one in the open air and the other in his chamber. The captain returned from his voyage, and even from another undertaken ten months afterwards: these two loaves were found equally good. This fact, which proves the benefits that may be derived from this bread, is preserved in the registers of the Royal Society of Agriculture at Rouen.

CHAPTER

CHAPTER VI.

OF THE COARSE FLOUR, SALEP, AND SAGO OF POTATOES.

BY giving directions how the Potatoe may be reduced into various forms, I do not pretend that it acquires at the same time all the medicinal qualities attributed to each of the substances with which I compare it; my intention is only to point out the wholesome resources which this root is capable of affording to man, in the state of disease, when these substances fail.

Of the Coarse Meal of Potatoes.

UNDER the name of *gruaux*, it is usual to comprehend the seeds of the grasses, grosly divided by mills, and freed in part from their cortical cover. The way of turning them to use resembles the original use of farinaceous substances in general;

ral; it confifts in diluting and boiling them in a nutritious vehicle. Now Potatoes, boiled or roafted, before they have been dried, cannot be brought under this denomination; they rather form a kind of falep, as I will foon fhew.

When the Potatoes have been cleaned and peeled, they fhould be fliced, and laid on fearces covered with paper, which are then to be placed in an oven: they very foon fhrink, lofe their tranfparency, and in twenty-four hours become friable enough to be broken to pieces by the action of the mill or peftle. When they are only bruifed, they may be diftinguifhed by the name of coarfe meal, and by that of flour, when reduced to a fine powder.

The flices, when dried, are wrinkled and tarnifhed at the furface, and internally whitifh: when you bite them, you think you have wheat or rye between your teeth: they are rather longer in boiling than the

roots

roots when whole and frefh; they befides have a dark grey colour, and their tafte is fomewhat different.

The flour obtained from dried Potatoes, is foft to the touch, but the colour is a dirty grey: if an attempt is made to form a ball of it with water, it acquires fcarce any tenacity; when diluted and boiled, like other kinds of coarfe meals, (fuch as oatmeal, &c.) in milk, broth, or any mucilaginous decoction, it diminifhes their tranfparency, affumes the confiftence of broth, emits an odour refembling that of pafte of flour, and its tafte is lefs agreeable than the Potatoe itfelf before it is dried.

It would be in vain to hope, that grinding and dreffing, which have fo much influence on the quality of flour, are capable of improving that of Potatoes; as the extractive matter which they contain, has not been combined by the operation of drying, it is fo far developed as to be very

very fenfible, both to the eye and the tafte, in every preparation into which it is introduced; either in wheaten bread, which it renders difagreeable and brown, or in porridge, which is of a yellow colour, and unpleafant tafte; it may indeed be corrected by fugar or aromatics.

From what has been faid, it appears that the flour of Potatoes fhould be diftinguifhed from the ftarch; fince the one is an approximation of the conftituent parts, in confequence of the evaporation of the aqueous fluid, whilft the other is one of the principles formed by vegetation, and very eafily feparable, provided thefe roots have not undergone the action of fire.

The flour of Potatoes may be long kept without alteration; it needs only to be fufficiently dried, and to be fecured from moifture, and the deftructive animals which it allures: it appeared to me quite as good, after a year had elapfed, as the firft first day of its preparation; nor could I ever perceive any appearances of germination, at the return of spring, or that it changed colour, as some have advanced, with a view, no doubt, of depreciating such kind of food.

It would be infinitely more expeditious to dry the Potatoes whole; but I have long since learned from experience, that however small they happened to be, it is impossible to dissipate the whole of the watery principle; they become soft, and spoil, sooner than part with the remaining moisture, which prevents their being reduced to powder. I have often exposed Potatoes to a heat of 100—120°, in order to prevent them from shooting or sprouting; this method effectually deprives them of this faculty, but at the same time greatly injures the organization; these roots, half dried, are not so delicate when boiled, and they cannot be long kept without suffering internally.

As it is very difficult to clean Potatoes, on account of their inequality, and to peel them raw, unlefs they have been foaked for fome time in water; the fmootheft may be felected for this purpofe, and the fkin may be taken off at the time of gathering: women and children may be charged with this tafk.

I must however obferve, that whatever care may be taken in culling, cleaning, drying, and grinding Potatoes, neither the coarfe meal nor the flour can ever be brought to poffefs every advantage; however you may prepare them, you muft not expect to have an aliment under this form as pleafant as it is wholefome; what a difference, when they are boiled before they are dried! Two products are obtained, which have nothing in common but the fame fource.

Of the Salep of Potatoes.

The bulbous roots of the family of orchis, when they have been boiled, cleaned, ed, dried, and reduced to powder, receive the name of salep; the use of this substance is well known, when we wish to procure a substantial and easily digestible nourishment. The Potatoe, subjected to the same preparation, resembles it so strongly, that it may not only be substituted in its stead on many occasions, but likewise, in case of want, supply the place of the fresh roots, till the next crop is ripe.

When Potatoes are nearly boiled, take them from the fire; peel, slice, and set them in or upon an oven after the bread has been drawn; in thirty hours they will be dried enough, and will have lost $\frac{3}{4}$ of their weight.

The trouble of slicing them, especially when it is proposed to reduce them to powder, may be avoided, by making the above-mentioned pulp, and spreading it in thin beds in a stove; but they should be be boiled and reduced to pulp only as they are dried, left they should turn four.

The Potatoe, by being boiled, sliced, and dried, acquires the transparency and hardness of horn; it breaks short, and the fracture is somewhat like that of glass; it does not attract the moisture of the atmosphere, is pounded with difficulty, and affords a dry whitish powder, resembling that of gum arabic: this powder dissolves in the mouth, and with water forms a mucilage. Such are the general properties of salep.

In Switzerland and Alsatia, an instrument contrived on purpose for breaking Potatoes has been used with advantage; it consists of a cylindrical pipe, pierced at the bottom with a number of small holes, like a skimmer, through which the Potatoes are forced, after they have been peeled, dried slowly, and boiled: thus a kind of vermicelli is formed; hence the Genoese and Italian pastes may be imitated, by by mixing the powder of Potatoes with the pulp, and adding the ufual feafoning. This mixture is eafily hardened, and fwells very well in hot water.

If the obfervations of Ellis and Magellan, on the antifcorbutic virtue of Potatoes, fhould be confirmed by further experiments; if this virtue, as there is every reafon to believe, refides in the extractive matter; thefe roots, which have loft nothing by being boiled and dried, will be more efficacious in this difeafe than the bread and bifcuit, that have been deprived in part of their extractive matter: they will have over frefh Potatoes the advantages of occupying lefs room, of being laid up any where, of keeping longer, and of becoming, in a moment's boiling, a wholefome and mild food, comparable to that of the Potatoe itfelf. The pulp ufed for making the bread, may be prepared in the moft dead feafon of the year; and this would be a fure mean of having thefe

roots

roots for food when they can no longer be had in fubftance.

Potatoes in falep do not, like the meal, alter the whitenefs of wheaten bread when they form a part of it, of different jellies or broths; they preferve their colour, tafte, and fmell, becaufe the extractive matter is confounded with the ftarch and parenchyma by boiling; whereas fimple deficcation acts on each of thefe principles feparately, and caufes an alteration, which makes dried Potatoes fo much inferior to thofe that have undergone a previous boiling.

When this falep is to be adminiftered, it fhould firft be reduced to a fine powder; an ounce of it fhould be boiled in an half-pint of water, for a quarter of an hour, and then paffed through a cloth; a little fugar and cinnamon fhould be added: when it grows cold, it becomes a whitifh kind of jelly, and fhould be given every two hours, in the dofe of one or two fpoonfuls,

fuls, according as the case requires. When it is proposed to make a mucilaginous ptisan, like rice or barley-water, the same quantity of salep may be diluted in a quart or three pints of water; it may be made pleasant by any syrup suited to the disease.

Here it will be objected, that my new salep is nothing but Potatoes, of which the different principles have been approximated by the evaporation of the excessive moisture; and that it cannot be considered as similar to a bulbous root, in which mucilage is extremely attenuated. I reply, that the boiling produces in the Potatoe a mucilage, on which the drying afterwards acts, by destroying the viscidity, and bringing it to the state of jelly. Besides, I have given it with advantage, in cases where salep was indicated, in bilious cholics, in diarrhœas, and in all diseases depending on acrimony of the lymph. But I do not wish to dogmatize in medicine, or to rob the rich of their salep, which

which cofts them 20 francs a pound: the expence of mine will be very trifling; and I may furely be allowed to call it the falep of the poor.

Of Sago of Potatoes.

Sago is well known to be a feculency, feparated by fearces, and wafhed from the farinaceous pith contained in certain palms, very common in the Molucca iflands. This feculency, which is not foluble in water unlefs it boils, which then increafes confiderably in bulk, and changes into a tranfparent jelly, is nothing but real ftarch. Now, as I think I have proved that this fubftance is identical, like fugar, in whatever body it may happen to be contained, the ftarch of Potatoes may fupply its place entirely.

The form of fmall grains, in which fago is imported, and the reddifh colour, are occafioned by the degree of heat employed by the Indians for drying it. The way

way to extract the starch from Potatoes has been already shewn; it would be possible to bring it to a perfect resemblance with sago, if it could be supposed that drying, carried to a great length, could at all influence its œconomical properties.

When sago of Potatoes is to be used, put a spoonful in a saucepan, and add gradually a pint of water, or milk; it should be set to boil over a slow fire, and stirred constantly for half an hour; sugar and aromatics may be added.

How many stomachs, naturally weak, or enfeebled by excess or disease, and incapable of digesting solid food, would be relieved and even cured by the use of salep and sago of Potatoes? Each affords a wholesome nutriment, easy of digestion, and adapted to fulfil the same indications as salep and sago properly so called. They are restoratives for convalescents, old persons, and children. The Tapioca of the Americans, which is nothing but the whitest

whiteſt and pureſt ſtarch of the magnoe, affords excellent and very wholeſome broths for debilitated and conſumptive patients.

Potatoes, I repeat it, may ſupply the place of ſalep and ſago, in times of plenty; two ſubſtances imported from very diſtant countries, and on that account liable to be ſuſpected of improper mixtures. If they are ſpecifics for our diſeaſes, their exorbitant price prevents the poor from profiting by them. The ſubſtitutes here propoſed will coſt almoſt nothing: four pounds of Potatoes afford one pound of ſalep; and ſix pounds, one of ſago.

Shall we for ever lay the two Indies under contribution to ſatisfy our principal wants, and value only what is imported from far, and has the merit of growing in another hemiſphere?

CHAPTER

CHAPTER VII.

OF THOSE FARINACEOUS SEEDS AND ROOTS FROM WHICH IT IS NECESSARY TO EXTRACT THE STARCH.

IT has been long a prevailing opinion, that feeds belonging to the great family of graffes, were the only receptacle of ftarch: but it cannot now be doubted, that it is to be found in pulfe, and in a great number of other feeds and roots belonging to various claffes. I would almoft venture to alledge, that there is no part of fructification in which it is not contained; that it is identical, from whatever fubftance it is extracted; and that the ftarch of feeds is not more attenuated than the ftarch of roots.

It feems to me that berries and ftone fruits cannot contain ftarch, becaufe their pulp is too foft to hold and fupport a folid body:

body: but my conjectures respecting apples, and other like fruits, were very different; for, as they are firmer, they may well serve such purposes: but my enquiries made with this view, were fruitless. M. Duval also suspected the same thing, in consequence of some experiments more successful than mine. We tried together, whether his suspicion was well founded, and we actually found starch in some sweetish cyder-apples, whilst others of a sourer taste did not afford an atom.

Starch then is contained not only in roots, bark, stalks, and seeds, but in fruits likewise: there remain only leaves and flowers, and I would not assert that it may not be found sometimes in them; and the rather, as I have examined, and obtained from several of them a mucilage nearly resembling it: then it may be said, that all the organs of plants are proper for the formation of starch as well as of sugar, two substances differing in their nature and properties.

As

As most of the following seeds and roots have never been thought to contain any alimentary principle, because it was not known that they contained starch; that starch was the essential part of farinaceous substances; and that it may be separated from the other parts, and reduced to the form of bread; they have always been ranked among poisonous substances: in which medicine has sought specifics, and the arts resources, which have not always been confirmed by observation and experiment.

As the extraction of the starch, and the way to mix it with a glutinous matter, in order to make real bread, by the help of fermentation and baking, have been described at great length already; it will be sufficient to recapitulate the most essential part here.

Take any of the following roots, when ripe, strip them of their skin, divide them by a grater, pour water on the grated mass, which,

which, as it paffes through a clofe fearce, will carry along with it a matter that will depofit itfelf gradually at the bottom of the wooden or earthen veffel fet to receive it: after fome time, pour off the liquor, and wafh the depofited matter repeatedly with frefh water, till it becomes perfectly infipid; then expofe it to the moft gentle heat; as it becomes dry, it turns white, and prefents a friable matter, without colour, tafte, or fmell, exhibiting all the characters that diftinguifh ftarch.

Of all the plants mentioned below, the root, or its bark, are the only parts proper for the object in view: it fhould be gathered in autumn, fhould be chofen frefh and fucculent, cleared from its hairy filaments and its coloured coats; it fhould alfo be cleaned and wafhed till the water appears quite tranfparent and colourlefs.

As all the bitternefs of the horfe-chefnut, the afperity of the acorn, the caufticity of the arum and ranunculufes, the burning acrimony

acrimony of the bryony, &c. remain in the water employed to feparate and wafh the ftarch, it is proper to ufe wooden inftruments to ftir the mixture, as the hands might fuffer.

The ftarch feparated from the feeds and roots mentioned below, when well wafhed and dried, is perfectly identical: but it is not fufficient to feparate it from the fubftance in which it is contained; it is moreover requifite to give directions how to convert it into food. It may be introduced, either alone or mixed with the pulp of Potatoes, into the dough of various grains, to make an addition to the quantity of bread. Bread may be made without flour of any kind, by the procefs defcribed above; but if the Potatoe fhould alfo fail, the pulpous fruits of the cucurbitaceous family, fuch as the pumpkin, which are fometimes added to wheaten dough in various proportions, may be fubftituted: laftly, fhould every other refource source fail, the starch representing flour would still serve for food; it would be sufficient to dilute it in some vehicle, in order to obtain a very nutritious broth or jelly.

I have used the several starches extracted from the following plants, without distinction, nor was it possible to tell from which it had been procured: when there is a slight difference perceptible in the taste, smell, or colour, it should be attributed to the number of washings rather than to any essential difference of nature.

The Horse-Chesnut *.
The Acorn.

[The roots only of the following vegetables afford starch in considerable quantity.]

---

* This is not an indigenous tree of this country, nor very often to be found in it. In France there are whole forests of it.

Common Burdock,	Arctium Lappa.
Deadly Nightshade,	Atropa Belladonna.
Bistort Snakeweed,	Polygonum Bistorta.
White Bryony,	Bryonia alba.
Meadow Saffron,	Colchicum autumnale.
Meadow-sweet,	Spiræa filipendula
Masterwort,	Imperatoria Ostruthium.
Black Henbane,	Hyoscyamus niger.
Pimpernel-leaved Dropwort, -	Œnanthe Pimpinelloides.
Obtuse-leaved Dock,	Rumex obtusifolius.
Sharp-leaved Dock,	Rumex acutus.
Water-Dock,	Rumex { Aquaticus an. Britannica?
Wake Robin,	Arum maculatum.
Bulbous Crowfoot,	Ranunculus bulbosus.
Knotted Figwort,	Scrophularia nodosa.
Dwarf Elder,	Sambucus ebulus.
Common Elder,	Sambucus nigra.
Common Flag,	Iris pseudacorus.
Stinking Flag,	Iris fœtidissima.

CHAPTER VIII.

A LIST OF SUCH FARINACEOUS SEEDS AND ROOTS AS MAY BE USED ENTIRE FOR FOOD.

ALL the parts of plants have a particular feason in which they may be gathered in their higheft perfection: fruits and feeds have generally no fixed period, but it is neceffary to wait till they are quite ripe: as to roots, opinions are yet divided with refpect to the time of gathering them: they are indeed fucculent in fpring; but it may at the fame time be remarked, that the liquid vehicle which then abounds, having not undergone a fufficient elaboration, is rather watery than mucilaginous; that part of this vehicle fhould acquire nutritive properties; and that thefe advantages cannot be had together, except at the decay or fall of the leaves: this confideration alone fhould make us give the preference

preference to the opinion of thofe who maintain that roots fhould be gathered in autumn.

But if it is neceffary to wait for this feafon, in order to collect the roots of the uncultivated plants to be mentioned below, how can they be diftinguifhed, fince at this time the leaves, which may ferve to point them out, are either withered or fallen? Moft of them may be gathered before their complete maturity. Befides, it is of fmall confequence whether they poffefs the whole quantity of ftarch which they have in autumn; the circumftances in which it is propofed to have recourfe to them admitting of no delay.

It may be added, that the farinaceous roots of perennial wild plants do not acquire their qualities, confiftence, and bulk, in the fpace of a fingle year; fome require a period of five or fix years to arrive at their entire perfection: it is evident, that in this cafe they will afford much more ftarch;

starch; which afterwards decreases as their fleshy state decays, and as they approach that period of old-age when they assume the consistence of woody fibres. All these reasons, deduced from experiment and observation, may serve as a proof that it is impossible to ascertain the quantity of starch that may be extracted from a given weight, and consequently the price of the food obtained from them: famine never calculates; and in times of scarcity, gold has scarce any value in comparison of bread.

If the starch contained in the seeds and roots of wild vegetables was always attended with poisonous juices or pulp, I should certainly continue to propose the extraction of it, in the way already described, because hitherto no better method of applying these plants to the purposes of food has been discovered; but happily there are also uncultivated plants, in which the several principles are as mild as starch, and which may be used for food without

without separating it. It is of importance to avoid loss when plenty fails, and advantage must be taken of every thing, in order to have necessaries. I only regret that such plants are less numerous and common than the others.

Wall Barley,	Hordeum murinum.
Cock's-foot Panick-grass,	Panicum Dactylon.
Wild Oat-grass,	Avena fatua.
Tall Oat-grass,	Avena elatior.
Floating Fescue-grass,	Festuca fluitans.
Annual Darnel-grass,	Lolium temulentum.

[The seeds of this grass should be exposed to the heat of an oven before they are taken to the mill; the bread should be well baked, and should not be eaten before it is cold. These simple precautions ought always to be observed when new grain is used; they would be the means of preventing the disorders so often prevailing in autumn, of which the real cause is frequently unknown.]

Field

Field Broomgrafs,　　　Bromus fecalinus.

[The fame precautions are neceffary to be taken with the feeds of this grafs as with thofe of the preceding.]

Cow Wheat,	Melampyrum arvenfe.
Cock's-comb,	Rhinanthus criftagalli.
Hare's-foot,	Trifolium arvenfe.
Corn Spurrey,	Spergula arvenfis.
Knot-grafs,	Polygonum aviculare.
Snakeweed,	Polygonum convolvulus.
Corn Cockle,	Agroftemma Githago.

THE SEEDS of the foregoing may be ufed for food, but it is from the ROOTS of the following plants that we are to derive the fame advantage.

Heath peafe,　　　Orobus tuberofus.

[The root and feeds may be ufed for food.]

Wild Carrot,　　　Daucus Carota.

Hare-bells,　　　Hyacinthus non-fcriptus.

[The roots of this plant are faid by fome

to have a poifonous quality, when newly gathered.]

Wild Parfnep,   Paftinaca fylveftris.
Pignut,   Bunium bulbo-caftanum.

CHAPTER IX.

A LIST OF WILD PLANTS, OF WHICH THE ROOTS MAY BE SUBSTITUTED IN THE PLACE OF POT-HERBS.

WILD Celery,	Apium paluftre.
Silver-weed,	Potentilla anferina.
Canterbury-bells,	Campanula trachelium.
Milk-thiftle,	Carduus marianus.
Globe-thiftle,	Carduus eriophorius.
Marfh-thiftle,	Carduus paluftris.
Wild Succory	Cichorium intybus.
Common Comfrey,	Symphitum officinale.
Alexanders	Smyrnium olufatrum.
White Water-lily,	Nymphæa alba.
Female Orchis,	Orchis morio.
Male Orchis,	Orchis mafcula.

Man Orchis, Orchis militaris.
Broad-leaved Orchis, Orchis latifolia.
Pyramidal Orchis, Orchis pyramidalis
Yellow Bethlem-ſtar, Ornithogalum luteum.

Let it not appear ſurprizing, that among the ſeaſonings which uncultivated vegetables are capable of affording, I do not enumerate any ſpecies of Fungus, though they all grow ſpontaneouſly on the hills, and in the woods and plains. Moſt of theſe ſingular plants contain a poiſon of great activity; and, unhappily, we are deficient both in chemical and botanical means to eſtabliſh certain marks of diſtinction between them, which may ſerve to characterize their effects, and at the ſame time prevent the fatal miſtakes every day made in chooſing them : it would then be better, as Geoffroy expreſſes it, to return muſhrooms reared in beds to the dunghill whence they ſprung.

Were it even in our power to render all muſhrooms innocent by any particular operation, experience proves that the beſt
ſorts,

forts, thofe ufually introduced into our ragouts, may become highly dangerous, either becaufe they have been gathered too early or too late, or in a bad feafon; or from having been expofed for a long time to fogs, the dew or the vapour of any putrefying fubftance; or laftly, by eating to excefs, or from the habit of body at the time of eating. M. DE JUSSIEU has told me, that both he and his uncles were well perfuaded that all mufhrooms were fufpicious. What more refpectable authority in botany can I quote in behalf of my opinion? How many accidents, that have happened immediately after meals, have been attributed to caufes totally different, while they were occafioned by an immoderate ufe of mufhrooms?

It would be in vain to hope that a fketch of the horrible but too certain picture of the victims daily facrificed by mufhrooms, would induce men to abandon them; gluttony would ftill prevail, and, though the moft ftriking inftances warn

warn us every moment of the poisonous principle contained in fungous plants, their reputation has not suffered, but we continue to eat them with equal pleasure and security. Hence, since on this occasion calamity has not rendered us wiser, I will point out with sorrow and reluctance some means of preventing or diminishing the accidents which arise from this source.

There should always be an interval between the gathering and eating of mushrooms, during which they should be soaked in cold water, and then blanched in fresh water; and wine, vinegar, lemon-juice, or acidulous plants, should be mixed with the dishes in which they are used. Lastly, it is of the highest importance to chew them well, lest the property belonging to several sorts, of swelling in the stomach, should give rise to enormous pieces, which would be pernicious solely on account of their indigestible bulk.

Mushrooms, I repeat it, are not nutritious;

tritious; they only contain a favoury fubftance, which may eafily be difpenfed with; and, fince there is no way to diftinguifh the mufhroom which is effentially poifonous, from that which may be rendered poifonous by a thoufand accidents, let us not hefitate to profcribe it from the clafs of feafonings, by fubftituting the heart of artichokes, celery, and the root of parfley, and other garden plants; in which it would be eafy, on enquiry, to difcover the feducing relifh of the deceitful mufhroom.

CHAPTER X.

TO MAKE A LIQUOR WHICH MAY BE SUBSTITUTED IN THE PLACE OF BEER.

IN order to obtain liquor which may be fubftituted in the place of beer, take rye or wheaten bran, and boil it in foft water;

water; then strain it, and fill a barrel with it; afterwards diffuse a leaven, eight days old, in it, and, if the weather is hot, fermentation will take place in less than twenty-four hours; as soon as the foam that arises through the bung-hole begins to sink, stop it up carefully, and let the liquor rest for some days, that it may become clear. When the bran has been hindered from acquiring any bad taste, this liquor is pleasant enough, has a vinous and acidulous taste; it is, in short, the lemonade of the poor inhabitants of the country.

So easily is water made to acquire vinous properties, and to quench thirst, that we need not rob the cattle of their bran; a little honey or sugar, a few saccharine roots diluted in a good deal of water, will suffice.

F I N I S.

www.ingramcontent.com/pod-product-compliance
Lightning Source LLC
Chambersburg PA
CBHW020304090426
42735CB00009B/1222